W9-BXM-200

OSCEOLA

MEMORIES OF A SHARECROPPER'S DAUGHTER

COLLECTED AND EDITED BY

ALAN GOVENAR

ILLUSTRATED BY

SHANE W. EVANS

JUMP AT THE SUN

HYPERION BOOKS FOR CHILDREN
NEW YORK

TO THE MEMORY OF CLARENCE MAYS,
AND FOR GENERATIONS TO COME
~A.G.

TO GOD,
AND MY BEST FRIENDS, KATE, TAYE,
AND OLUBAYO
~S.W.E.

Text copyright © 2000 by Alan Govenar and Osceola Mays.
Illustrations copyright © 2000 by Shane W. Evans.
For information address Hyperion Books for Children,
114 Fifth Avenue, New York, New York 10011-5690.
First Edition
Designed by Christine Kettner
3 5 7 9 10 8 6 4
Printed in Singapore.

LIBRARY OF CONGRESS CATALOGING-IN-PUBLICATION DATA
Mays, Osceola, 1909–
Osceola : memories of a sharecropper's daughter / collected and edited by Alan Govenar; illustrated by Shane W. Evans.—1st ed.
p. cm.
Summary : A sharecropper's daughter describes her childhood in Texas in the early years of the twentieth century.
ISBN 0-7868-0407-6 (hardcover : alk. paper).— ISBN 0-7868-2357-7 (lib. bdg.)
1. Mays, Osceola, 1909– —Interviews—Juvenile literature. 2. Mays, Osceola, 1909–—Childhood and youth—Juvenile literature.
3. Afro-American women—Texas—Harrison County—Interviews—Juvenile literature.
4. Afro-American women—Texas—Harrison County—Biography—Juvenile Literature. 5. Afro-Americans—Texas—Harrison County—
Interviews—Juvenile literature. 6. Afro-Americans—Texas—Harrison County—Social life and customs—Juvenile literature.
7. Sharecropping—Texas—Harrison County—History—20th century—Juvenile literature. 8. Harrison County (Tex.)—Biography—
Juvenile Literature. [1. Mays, Osceola, 1909–. 2. Afro-Americans—Biography. 3. Women—Biography.]
I. Govenar, Alan B., 1952–. II. Evans, Shane, ill. III. Title.   F392.H39 M35   2000
976.4 ` 19200496073 ` 092—dc21 [B]   98-40411

Illustrations on pages 4 and 54 are based on photographs by Alan Govenar.
The audio tape *Osceola Mays : Spirituals and Poems*, and the video *Osceola Mays : Stories, Songs, and Poems*, are available
from Documentary Arts, P.O. Box 140244, Dallas, Texas 75214.

Visit www.jumpatthesun.com.

ACKNOWLEDGMENTS

In making this book, I have been helped by many people. I extend my deepest appreciation to Osceola Mays, who generously shared her memories with me.

I am also grateful to Verna Raven, who introduced me to Osceola in 1983, Harry and Gleniece Robinson, Dolly Taylor, Reverend C. A. W. Clark, Sr., and the members of the Good Street Baptist Church, who supported my efforts early on; my wife, Kaleta Doolin, who offered insight as this work evolved; my daughter, Breea, who listened intently as I read aloud many of these stories for the first time and continues to talk about their lasting impressions; and my son, Alex, whose curiosity for history and its meaning has furthered my understanding of the importance of the spoken word.

INTRODUCTION

SCEOLA MAYS sits alone on the couch in her living room. She rolls her eyes upward and smiles. Then she begins to sing. The words come forth with a heartfelt cadence. Her body sways forward. The notes are long and deep, flattened in a style she learned from her mother, Azalean Douglas, and her grandmother, Laura Walker, who was ten years old when the Emancipation Proclamation was signed to end slavery.

The light from the window behind her casts shadows of the barbed wire strung across the glass as a burglar deterrent. "In South Dallas lots of people walk the street day and night," Osceola explains. "So far, there hasn't been any serious trouble. A couple of years ago I used to hear people shooting off guns on Saturday night, but the police came out and closed them down. These days I just watch and pray. A portion of my life I like better here than where I grew up [in the East Texas town of Waskom], but a part of me misses the country. That was my home."

Osceola moved to Dallas in 1945. She did odd jobs, working in a drugstore and a laundry, but mostly, in the homes of white people as a nanny and domestic. "I've had a hard life, but the stories and songs and poems I learned as a young girl kept me going. I lay down in bed at night and think about them. Sometimes I sing to myself."

This book is an oral history, pieced together from interviews and conversations I've had with Osceola over the last fifteen years. In the book, I have tried to preserve Osecola's oral style by staying as close as possible to the audio recordings I made with her. I involved Osceola in the process of editing the texts by comparing the different versions and discussing them. The time frame of the book focuses on the part of her life that she remembers most, from her earliest memories at age three to her graduation from high school and the first years of marriage and work. These texts are a vital part of Osceola's everyday life. She recalls them with a sincere pride for her friends and family, as well as for students in her Sunday School class at the Good Street Baptist Church in Dallas.

Over the last decade, Osceola's audience has grown. She has participated in Folk Artists in Schools residencies and has performed in numerous programs at the Dallas Folk Festival, the Dallas Black Academy of Arts and Letters, and the African American Museum. In 1989, Osceola participated in a touring program I organized called "Texas in Paris," presented at the Centro Flog in Florence, Italy, and the Maison des Cultures du Monde in Paris, France.

The memories of Osceola Mays express the sorrows and joys of three generations of African Americans and demonstrate the strength of the oral tradition. In African cultures, oral history has traditionally been passed on from one generation to the next. Active tradition bearers, often known as *griots*, are celebrated for their ability to recount the stories of their people. Osceola, in her own way, is a griot, a matriarch, who embraces the legacy of her mother and grandmother. Through these life experiences, history becomes personal. The harsh realities of segregation and discrimination are offset by the vitality of family and community. Together, the texts combine oral history and tradition with the natural power of language and inspiration.

—Alan Govenar

MY HOMETOWN

THE SHORTCUT to my house was a pig trail. I was born on a rural route outside of Waskom, Texas, outside of Marshall, on Wednesday, December 13, 1909. Waskom had a small population. In the city limits there might have been 250 people living there, but we lived out on Rural Route 1. I think there were about 135 mail stops on the rural route. Each box had a number on it, and ours was 129.

In Waskom, there were two general stores, a little cafe, one furniture store, one big grocery store, one clothing store, one cotton gin, and two medical doctors—Herbert Vaughn and Olden Abney—they each had their own office.

I lived on a dirt road where the other black folks lived. The white folks lived within the city limits of Waskom. Everything was segregated. We had our own schools and our own churches. We lived apart, separated from white folks in just about everything we did.

We were poor. I never did see any cars. The mail carrier

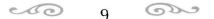

came around in a two-wheeled jig [a small wagon with one seat] drawn by one horse.

We lived in a small weathered-wood frame house. It didn't have any paint on it. There was no window glass; we had windows that had little doors of wood that opened and closed. We had one bedroom and one kitchen and a front porch. We had two beds. The children slept in one bed and Mama and Daddy slept in the other. There wasn't any electricity or running water. We'd get water from the well or we'd use the spring water that came up out of the ground.

How I Got My Name

WHEN I WAS A LITTLE GIRL, maybe three or four years old, there was an Indian man traveling through Waskom. He stretched his tent right close to our house. Mama and Daddy would drink coffee with him. Sometimes he'd give me some cookies and candy, and my brother, Reginald, got some, too. And I told Mama I wanted to be named for him.

Mama said, "No."

"Well," he said, "that's all right. She can wear my name."

And I named myself Osceola. That was his name, and my name was after him.

Up until then, they called me Garnell, after a little white girl down in the neighborhood. She was Mr. B. Folsom's daughter. White folks just liked for black folks to be named after them, I guess. It was a carryover from slavery days, when slaves were given the names of their masters.

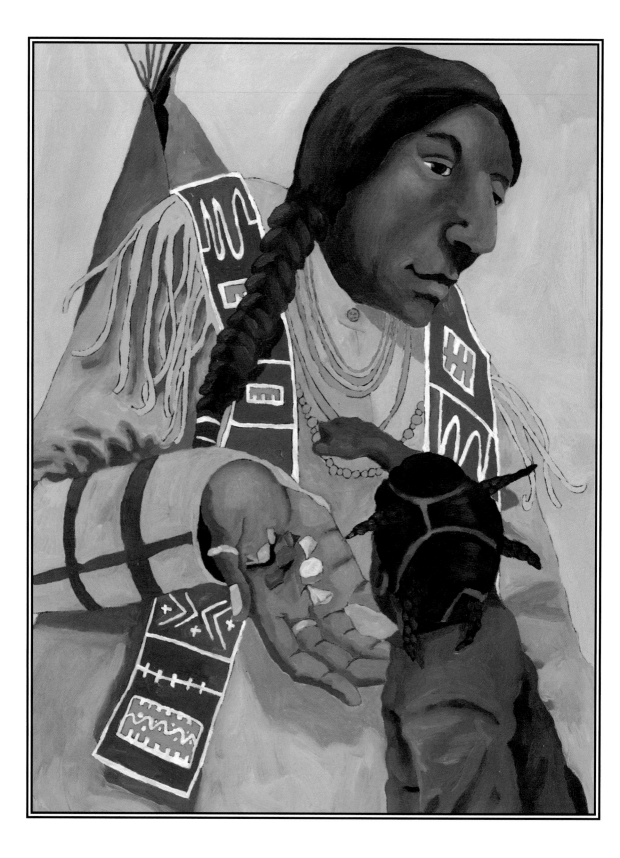

Reginald was named for a white man who lived close by us. He lived in a big house. And my cousin had three children named for white folks. But my mama and daddy didn't call me Garnell too much. They just called me "Sister."

I didn't want to be named Garnell. I wanted to be named Osceola after that man who gave me some goodies. But then he took down his tent and went on to someplace else. I never saw him again, but I got his name.

DADDY'S WORK

MY DADDY WAS a sharecropper, meaning he'd make a crop and then he'd have to share it with the white man who owned the land. The white man would give my daddy one third and he'd keep two thirds. My daddy worked hard in the cotton fields. He had to plow the land, put down the fertilizer, plant the seeds, and keep cultivating the crops until they were ready to harvest. Then he kept the garden for the white people.

But when the crops failed, it didn't leave us much to live on. We had a little garden with vegetables—tomatoes, sweet potatoes, peppers, cabbage, turnips, okra, collards, mustard greens, squash, and green beans. In the winter, we milked the white man's cows and he'd let us keep some of the milk.

I didn't ever see my daddy with any money. The boss man would give him something called "brozine," which was worth money. He could use it in a little store that the boss man owned. He could go there and get groceries for the family. Brozine was like dimes, quarters, and nickels. But they were just metal coins—lightweight coins. I don't remember any real money at all.

The white folks would give Daddy a pair of shoes so that he could work, and they gave him clothes in the winter. But he'd have to buy us shoes and clothes in the commissary with whatever brozine he had. Then, Daddy would work that big crop, and when the crop was made, the boss man would say, "Well, you didn't clear any money."

In the wintertime, he had to get extra work other places—cut wood for the cotton gin, make cross ties for the railroad track, stuff like that. That's what a man had to do to make extra money. But in the spring and summer, when the crop was coming up, they'd let Daddy get plenty of food so he could work long and hard.

THE DAY I WAS BAPTIZED

MOST BLACK FOLKS I grew up with went to the Boggy Bayou Baptist Church. I loved going to church every week, singing the songs, like "I'm Going Down to the Big Baptizing" and "Amazing Grace." And I liked to hear the Bible stories about David and Moses and Peter and Jonah and the Whale. Mama used to tell me these Bible stories. And she made me learn them, too.

In those days they didn't baptize little babies. I was eight years old when I got baptized in a pond close to Bayou Creek near the church. The preacher would baptize children once a year, in August on the fourth Sunday. The preacher who baptized me was Mount Moore. He put on a long robe and went out in the water with two helpers, one to bring the children out into the water, and one to stand there with him to help baptize the children one at a time. Sometimes, the children saw snakes bobbing their heads above the water, and then going back

under the water, only to come up at a different place. Two or three of the children might be screaming, and the preacher said, "Don't worry about those snakes. They won't bother you because God is here to protect you. Can't you trust God? God will take care of you."

The preacher would immerse each child in the water and then he'd bring them up. He'd say, "Everybody sing, 'I'm So Glad I Got My Religion in Time.'" Then each child was taken back to shore, where they were met by their mother and some other helpers, who took the child to a little building nearby to get dressed.

I was baptized in a red dress. I was so glad. Mama told me I was going to be an angel someday if I got baptized, and I wanted to be an angel. And I didn't mind getting wet because Mama had another dress ready for me to wear.

LEARNING ABOUT
WHITE FOLKS

I WAS NEVER AROUND white folks much when I was growing up. Mostly, we stayed at home.

I was about eight years old when I started to understand what the old people were saying. Everywhere I went, they would talk real softly so nobody could hear them, especially around the white folks, because they were still afraid of what might happen to them. I heard that the white folks would take people and burn them, and cut their feet off. These kind of stories made me scared to sleep.

· · · · ·

When I was about nine years old, Dr. Olden Abney, a white doctor, asked Mama if I could stay with him and help his wife around the house in the kitchen.

Mama said, "No, she too little. She don't know what she's doing."

Then he begged Mama, and Mama said, "I'm sick. I need

my girl to help with what little she can do."

I didn't want to stay to work, but I wanted to stay and eat that good food they gave me. I told Mama, "I want to stay."

And Mama said, "No, you can't stay."

So Mama kicked me on the foot, made me hurt for saying I was going to stay.

Mama said, "She can stay here for a while, but I'm going to come back and get her, Doctor."

Then she kicked me on the foot again and I said, "I don't want to stay. I want to go home with my mother."

If Mama hadn't given me that sign, I'd have stayed and ended up working for them.

. . . . .

Sometimes when my mother went to town, she'd say, "Every time I go to town, the white man kicks my dog around. It makes no difference that it's a hound, he better stop kicking my dog around."

We'd say it, too, behind the house, but Mama told me to hush because she thought we might say it around some white people and they might get us in trouble.

FEAR

WHEN I WAS A GIRL, Mama used to go to work in the field. And I was so afraid of white people that me and my little brother, we'd get under the bed when we heard the mail carrier come by. He was a white man. We'd hear him carry the mail in a two-wheel buggy or maybe on horseback called the Pony Express. And we'd run and get under the bed, stay under the bed, scared to move.

And when Mama and Daddy came, we didn't want to open the door to let them in because we thought he might be coming back at us.

One time the mail carrier passed in his buggy and we started running to get the mail out of the box and he told us, "Get back to the house! Don't ever come here again when I'm putting mail in the box."

We ran back into the house and stayed. We didn't get any mail out of the box that day. We didn't get any mail, not until

Mama came and got it. We were scared to death. People told us so many things about what white people did.

If anyone around Waskom got out of the rules and regulations of the white people, the mob would come and get them. They had to run to another state to get away. I didn't know the Ku Klux Klan, but I think the "mob" was the same thing. The mob would come on horses. If some Negro had done something they didn't like, and they said the "mob" crowd was coming, they'd go and hide down in the woods or go visiting somebody else's house. They wouldn't stay home that night.

Anybody died or got killed in the neighborhood, that was sad, sad news. Most of the older people didn't want children to know everything, and children didn't know very much in those days. We had to learn it in our own way. Go inside and get a drink of water, listen as they talk things over real low. We didn't stop walking because if we did, they'd stop.

STORIES ABOUT SLAVERY

MY GRANDMOTHER and Lucy Lewis were the first ones to tell me about the days of slavery. Lucy Lewis was a woman in the neighborhood who everyone called Aunt Lucy.

My grandmother's name was Laura Walker. She wore the slave owner's name. She said she was ten years old at the close of slavery, when she went back to her parents in Texas from South Carolina, where she had lived since she was a child, where she had lived since she was sold.

My grandmother told me that she was a real good girl and never got a whipping when she was under the care of her mistress and master, but a lot of girls got many a hard whipping until their backs were bloody and scarred.

All of the slave children ate from an old wood trough that was hewn from the woods. They'd boil the greens and peas for the field hands, then pour off the juice for the children.

· · · · ·

Aunt Lucy Lewis said that when she was a girl slave, she had to eat food out of the dish with the cats. She let the cats eat first, and then she ate after the cats were finished. If she didn't do it, she was whipped with many stripes. And sometimes her mistress would take that food and smear it on Aunt Lucy's face and she had to wear it all day because she was afraid to wash it off.

· · · · ·

The slaves sang songs to give hints to the others to escape. And the slave owners didn't mind them singing, but Mama told me they didn't know the hints that were in the lyrics to the songs: "Nobody Knows the Trouble I Seen," "Run, Sinner, Run," "I'm So Glad Trouble Don't Last Always," and "Swing Low, Sweet Chariot."

If the slave was smart, he'd catch the hints. Some might sing, "If you get there [meaning freedom] before I do, tell my friends, I'm coming, too." Another was "Run, sinner, run, and hunt you a hiding place," and "Soon one morning I'm going home to be free" and "Some day I'm going to lay down this heavy load." Had the slave owner known what they were talking about, he would have whipped them with many stripes.

THE CIVIL WAR

WHEN I WAS ABOUT NINE, my grandmother taught me a poem called "The Civil War." She put it together because she wanted me to learn about the Civil War and how black folks fought for their country. My grandmother was strict. I had to listen to her when she was talking.

> In the beginning of the Civil War
> the white man begin it
> but before the war was over
> the Black man was in it.
> At the Battle of San Juan Hill
> the Roughriders they begin it
> but before the battle was over
> the Black man was in it.
> Parker knocked the assassin down
> and to beat him he begin it

but before that fight was over
the Black man was in it.
White man, stop lynchin' and burnin' this Black race,
tryin' to thin it.
If you go to heaven or hell
you'll find a Negro in it.
Some time they pay us to swear or lie in court,
both black and white will do it,
but the truth will shine till the end of time
you'll find a Negro in it.

FREEDOM

WHEN THE NEGROES were set free, they made up a lot of little songs and verses. We would hear the old people saying them. I was learning them all the time.

After slavery was over, the black man knew he didn't have to go back to the field and work. He'd say:

> *One, two, three, look at me,*
> *the white folk mad*
> *because the black folks are free.*
> *I chew my 'bacco and spit my juice*
> *I'd go to the field but it ain't no use.*

I didn't hear a whole lot of people saying this, but I did hear it from Daddy's sister, Fannie Moore. She was smiling. It was tradition. She'd get so tickled when she said it. She'd laugh out loud and say, "We're not so free. We've got a long way to go yet."

One woman, one black woman said:

> *Free at last, free at last.*

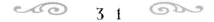

Thank God almighty
I'm free at last.
Freedom, freedom
oh, freedom for me.
Before I be a slave
I be buried in my grave
and I'll go home
to my Lord to be saved.
When I was a slave
I fell on my knees and prayed
that I might be free someday.
The Lord heard my cry so strong
I'll go home to my Lord and be saved.

I think I first heard "Free at Last" from my daddy's sister, George Ana Richmond. I don't know where she got it from, but it might have been from her mother, Laura. This one I heard often. People would make it into a song.

JUNETEENTH

JUNETEENTH was the day the slaves in Texas were told that they were free. June 19, 1865.

Every year on Juneteenth we'd celebrate; the white folks would let the black folks off from the field—no hoeing cotton or corn, no chopping cotton on that day, no plowing. The mules would stay in the pasture. All the black families would celebrate. We'd have a lot of foods that we didn't have every day like barbecue beef and pork. My grandmother would make tea cakes, gingerbread, and molasses bread. My daddy would buy a lot of red soda pop and they'd make homemade ice cream. We'd have a picnic and eat watermelons that we raised on the farm. And there'd be a barrel of lemonade.

The neighborhood would come together at the picnic grounds close to Waskom town. It had a building that we could use called Plantation Hall. We'd play baseball and have footraces. The fastest runner would get a prize of a dime or maybe a quarter, and the person who could throw a baseball the

farthest won a couple of apples. A dime in them days could buy what a dollar can buy now. Some of the men would ride horses that had never been ridden before. They'd break them on Juneteenth. Everybody had a good time, laughing and talking, and celebrating the day the slaves were told they were free.

TAP IT OUT
TO REMEMBER

I DIDN'T START TO LEARN until my mama told me that if I didn't, she was going to make me. "Don't ever forget, because you might need what I tell you one day. Someday it might be something great for you." Then she started telling me what I should know.

After we got through with lunch, my mother would sit us on the front porch and read from the Bible.

She'd tell me, "Listen to this. I'm not going to be here always."

And I'd sit there on the floor and just listen. Then Mama would sing and tell stories. When I was real small, she'd say little rhymes, and later on she'd recite poems.

My mama and grandma would sing all the time. We'd have

people in those days singing a mile away. They'd sing loud through the fields. All they had to make music was their mouths.

I remember the way things sound. Anything I want to remember, I'll name something that just sounds like that. Sometimes I tap it out to remember.

THE WAR IS ON

I WAS JUST A LITTLE GIRL when World War I broke out, but Mama told me about it in a poem:

> The War is on,
> the War is on.
> Everybody get ready
> for the War is on.
> In Nineteen and Seventeen on April the eight
> the War was declared in the United State.
> The United State said we all agree
> we have a nation that can rule the sea.
> The War is on,
> the War is on.
> Let everybody get ready
> for the War is on.
> The United State and her many friends
> met in a council face to face.
> They said all we want is a possible chance

to go to Germany to sell the case.
The War is on,
the War is on.
Let everybody get ready
for the War is on,
The United State and her many
    friends
said come all the world
God is on our side,
we're going to show Germany
    what we mean,
we're going to sink their
    submarines.
The War is on,
the War is on.
Let everybody get ready
for the War is on.
Go tell Billy Kaiser what Woodrow Wilson said.
He was not going to stop fighting
till they killed him dead.
Go ring the Liberty Bell
and give old Kaiser room in hell.
After a few weeks of fighting hard
Billy Kaiser's flag had fell.
The War is on,
the War is on.
Let everybody get ready
for the War is on.

GILLIAM'S STORM

I WAS ALMOST SIX when I learned "Gilliam's Storm." Mama told me the poem, and Daddy liked to make it into a song. I don't remember the storm, but I know the poem. Mama and Daddy used to live there in Gilliam, Louisiana. They said that Gilliam was wicked because there was only one church house in the town and the people there weren't very nice to the black folks.

> *Wasn't that a mighty time*
> *wasn't that a mighty time*
> *when the storm struck Gilliam town?*
> *Gilliam town was such a wicked town*
> *there wasn't but one church house in Gilliam town.*
> *It seemed like all the people there had laid God's*
>   *army down.*

Late one Wednesday evening the clouds rose
    dark and blue.
People were running and crying,
"Lord, Lord, what can I do?"
Oh, that was a mighty time
when the storm struck Gilliam town.
The cloud started toward
    Shreveport, Louisiana,
but God turned that cloud around
because He knew some Christians
    and sinners lived in Shreveport
    town.
Oh, wasn't that a mighty time
oh, wasn't that a mighty time
when the storm struck Gilliam town.
A woman said to her husband
I believe that cloud is about gone

God works in mysterious ways
His wonders to perform
He plants his footstep on the sea
and rides out on the storm.
Oh, that was a mighty time
when the storm struck Gilliam town.

SANTA CLAUS NIGHT

O N SANTA CLAUS NIGHT I was happy. I knew I was going to get a present. I'd hang a stocking up on the fireplace and I knew Santa Claus was going to put something inside: apples and oranges and a piece of candy—or maybe a little doll with a head out of china and the body and arms and legs made out of cloth.

When I was four or five, my mama bought me a big doll with curls—it was a white baby. We didn't have any black dolls back then. Still, I was so excited to get this doll baby. She had light brown hair and the curls were big and thick. And she had a plain gingham dress and a matching bonnet. She had on white socks and black shoes with one strap across each foot and one button on each side.

I only got two dolls on Santa Claus Night my whole life. One was china and the other was this baby with the curls. All the other dolls I had were homemade. In those days, people would

get flour in cloth bags and a doll might be drawn on the outside of the bag. And Mama would cut out that flour sack doll and sew it together. She'd take the two pieces and sew it together and stuff it with cotton.

I just loved my toys when I was little and I still love them. I only remember getting three toys in all those years—two dolls and a little cookstove made out of tin. It was painted with red and white checks. It had little tin pans and little tin pots.

My mama and daddy and all the old people told me to be good on Santa Claus Night. And on Christmas Day we'd eat pound cake and drink lemonade and sweet milk. Then they talked about Jesus because Christmas Day was Jesus' birthday. They said Jesus was Mary's baby. And I remember asking if Jesus was still a baby and they said he had grown up to be a man like Daddy. Later on, they'd read me stories about Jesus from the Bible. And they liked to sing spirituals and church songs.

MAMA DIES

MAMA SAID she was going to leave me. But I didn't believe her. I was too young to really know. I was only ten years old when she went away in childbirth. The baby was three days old and Mama died, leaving two boys and one girl. After a couple of weeks, I really began to miss Mama and realized she wasn't coming back.

I had some bad times after my mama died. My daddy went to West Texas to look for work and left me with his oldest sister. And she had three kids and the youngest was eleven and she wasn't nice to me. She'd treat me bad. When she had other girls come over to play, she'd tell them, "Don't play with her."

And my aunty gave me some new clothes and my cousin took them away and threw them in some high weeds away from the house and I couldn't find them. My aunty was going to whip me if I didn't find them, and I couldn't find them. My cousin said if I gave her some candy, she'd help me find my clothes.

And I gave her some candy, and as I was peeping out the window, she went out way back there and got the clothes. I watched where she got them.

I lived with them a year in Waskom on a rural route until my daddy came back and married again and we moved to Jewella, Louisiana. And I felt more welcome with my stepmother, because in my aunty's house I didn't get enough food to eat.

Santa Claus didn't come to me anymore after Mama died. Every year I got one present until Mama died and then I didn't get any more. My daddy didn't give me any presents after Mama died. He'd just give me fruit and candy.

MY STEPMOTHER

MY STEPMOTHER'S NAME was Gertrude Moore and she had children with my daddy. She had two boys and four girls.

I had a good stepmother. She took me on a train ride with her little babies every month. And we'd go to Waskom to see my step-aunties and my step-uncles.

I got to spend the night at my step-uncle's house, and his wife would cook tea cakes and a lot of good food. I felt so welcome, and every weekend after we moved back to Waskom from Louisiana, I enjoyed my stepfamily more than my own kinfolk.

My stepmother would make me a dress every Christmas. My favorite dress was a candy-striped dress, red and white, that she gave me when I was about twelve years old.

Every year she'd make me a dress, but I didn't get any toys. I never did get any toys until I was old enough to buy them for

myself. I guess I was about seventeen. That's why I like toys so much now.

I like little dolls and little wagons because I wanted them when I was a child—wagons, cars, trucks, anything with little wheels.

S C H O O L

HEN I WENT to school and made good grades, I was happy. I didn't want to be in the same grade two times.

Every day when I went to school, I remembered stories and poems that Mama taught me. I would say poems over and over to myself, that way Mama was always with me. Mama loved poems and I wanted to keep them alive after she had passed on.

When I was about eleven or twelve or thirteen, it made me proud to recite poems in school. Every Friday I'd stand up in class and say poems. All of the other children liked them so much that I started to write them myself.

In the eighth grade I wrote "On the Field of the Future," about doing the best you can with what you have.

MULTIPLY
BY
5
5 × 1 = 5
5 × 2 = 10
5 × 3 = 15
5 × 4 = 20
5 × 5 = 25
5 × 6 = 30
5 × 7 = 35
5 × 8 = 40
5 × 9 = 45
5 × 10 = 50
DIVIDE
111.14
7 | 778.00
7
07
7
08
7
10
7
30
28
2

They tell me you're going away, my friend,
away from home and all,
out on the field of the future
to play a life game of ball.
They tell me too that you are one and twenty,
but you don't look as old as that.
You look just young and slendered enough
to handle life's ball and bat.
Though I may be a little foggy
or old-timey, it don't matter much
what I say, but I'd like to give you
a little advice about the game
you're about to play.
Now when you play a game, play it well.
When you play a game,
play it with all your might,
the game half-played is never done right.
When you hit the ball, hit it on the head,
strike with all your might while the iron is red.
When there is work to do,
do it with all your might,
for things half-done
are never done right.

BLUES

WHEN I WAS A GIRL on the farm, I could hear them men in the fields, going through the woods singing blues. "You never miss your water until your well is gone dry. You never miss your baby till she says good-bye."

The old folks said that blues was the "devil's music." My grandma told me, "Stay away from them blues," and I did. But some of them blues have some real meaning to them.

The sun is going to shine in my back door one day.

I remember them songs, not all of them, but enough that it makes me happy to think of them.

Ain't but one thing that give a woman the blues—
when she don't have a bottom on her last pair of shoes.

The blues ain't nothing but a good man feeling bad,
blues is the worst thing a good man ever had.

I liked the sound of blues and the way the singers put words together. Some of those were true words about life.

I remember listening to blues on a record player. We didn't have a record player, but one of our neighbors did. That's when I first heard Blind Lemon Jefferson. He sang: "I'm broke and I ain't got a dime . . . Everybody get some hard luck some time."

A lot of them blues are like poetry. Blues was an inspiration to me when I heard them on that record player, even though the old folks didn't want us to listen to them.

THE BLACK MAN'S PLEA FOR JUSTICE

WHEN I GOT OLDER, I started liking the poems by E. D. Tyler. He was a minister in Louisiana, and he wrote poems. "The Black Man's Plea for Justice" was one of his poems I saw in a book. I never owned the book, but I read from it. And I remembered what he wrote, but I changed it up a little bit to make it my own. "The Black Man's Plea for Justice" was my favorite because it was about the history of black folks and their struggle for fair treatment.

THE BLACK MAN'S PLEA FOR JUSTICE

Hear me, statesman,
I am pleading to defend
the black man's cause.
Will you give me the protection
to outline your laws?

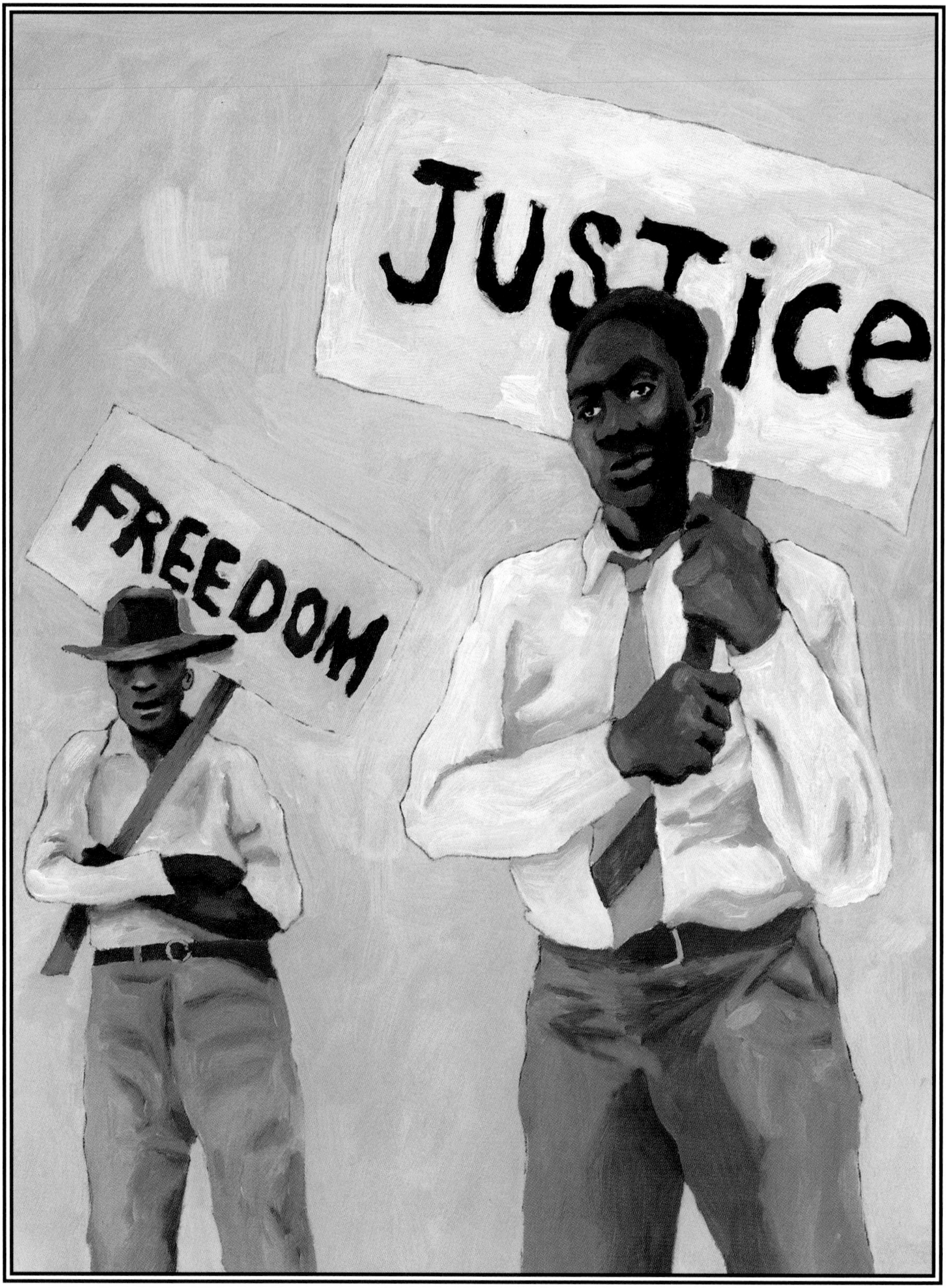
JUSTICE
FREEDOM

Will your lawyers plead my cases
in your courts?
Am I not a citizen?
Will you recognize my votes?
I pay dear for transportation
over all your railroad track.
I come up to every requirement
and I always pay my tax.
And when I don't fill in blanks correctly,
will you kindly teach me how?
Ruling power of this nation,
will you give me justice now?
I prepared your wedding supper
and I dug your father's grave.
I did everything you asked me
just because I was your slave.
I helped to build your great bridges
and I laid your railroad steel.
Oh, I been a mighty power
in your great financial wheel.
And when I don't do jobs correctly
will you kindly teach me how?
Ruling power of this nation
will you give me justice now?
I plowed your mules
I kept your rules
I fed and milked your cows
I kept my every vow.

I scraped the dirty mud from your shoes
I walked in snow to carry your news;
though I was not allowed to pray
because you guarded me every day.
I worked your fields
I prepared your meals—
and when I don't feed dogs and cats correctly,
will you kindly teach me how?
Ruling power of this nation
will you give me justice now?

GROWING UP AND MOVING ON

I WENT THROUGH the eleventh grade. Black schools where I lived didn't have a twelfth grade. After you finished the eleventh grade in Waskom, you had to go to work. My mama used to tell me, "When you wash them clothes, you wash them clean, because one day you may be working for white people—and if you don't wash them clean and nice, they will let you go." I'd be so tired of her telling me that, because I never thought I'd be doing that for a living. But when I grew up, that's what I had to do, just like my mama and grandma. I watched the children. I did the dishes, cleaned, things like that.

Then, when I wasn't working, I started liking boys, and boys would come see me. I was getting grown. I kind of lost interest in poems. I'd go to ball games and picnics. And I'd go to the store and buy ice cream. All these things took my mind off poems.

I married a man named Clarence Mays. He was a hard-

working man, a sharecropper just like my daddy. And he had a daughter named Loretha, and I became her stepmother. I loved that girl like my own.

In 1945, we left Waskom for good. We moved to Dallas to find better work. Clarence did whatever he could, working in a laundry and doing other odd jobs. And I took care of children and worked as a maid.

We had a good life together. We were married almost fifty years. Clarence died one month before our fiftieth wedding anniversary, November 20, 1985. He took good care of me.

Now I live by myself, but I don't mind. I go to church and see my family who I got left—Loretha's daughter, Caroline, and her husband, Ben, and their children, and my sister, Hattie White. Another sister, Mamie Douglas, still lives in Waskom, and another sister, Georgia Perkins, lives in Houston. I don't have any folks left by Daddy's first family; these sisters were born to my stepmother.

A SECRET JOY

AS THE YEARS go by, I think more of the poems and stories Mama and Grandma told me. I never did write them down. When I learned them, I didn't have any need to write them down. I didn't get but one pencil and I had to save that for school. But I promised myself I wouldn't forget them.

I remember all the things that meant the most to me—like Fridays that were my special day at school when I could say my poems out loud. And I remember other things that happened to me. I've had a hard time, but I made the best of it.

I kept these stories and poems with me and they gave me a secret joy. I'd say them to myself when I was working. I'd think of those things that Mama and Grandma said and I'd think of the stories and poems that I made up as I went along. I still say them to myself.

Sometimes, I wish I never stopped writing poems. If I had kept working, I would have been a good poem writer by now.